Faithful Friend

The Story of
Florence Nightingale

Faithful Friend

The Story of Florence Nightingale

Beatrice Siegel

SCHOLASTIC INC.
New York Toronto London Auckland Sydney

Photo Credits

Front cover and title page courtesy of Culver Pictures, Inc. Pages 3, 14, 31, 35, 71, 73, 91, 101, 103, and 117, courtesy of the New York Public Library Picture Collection. Pages 5, 47, 49, 57, 62, and 82 courtesy of the Bettmann Archive. Pages 10, 40, 54, 60, and 67, courtesy of the Historical Pictures Service, Chicago. Pages 19, 30, 96, and 109 courtesy of Bettmann/Hulton. Pages 21, 39, 86, 113, and 115 courtesy of the Florence Nightingale Museum Trust. Pages 23, 64, and 79 courtesy of The Granger Collection. Page 119 courtesy of UPI/Bettmann.

ISBN 0-590-43210-9

12 11 10 9 8 7 6 5   3 4 5 6/9

Printed in the U.S.A.   40

First Scholastic printing, March 1991

To Jane and Ned

Contents

Acknowledgments

Most of my research for this book was done at the Special Collections, Milbank Memorial Library, Teachers College, Columbia University, and I would like to express my appreciation to David M. Ment, Head, Special Collections, and Lucinda Manning, Manuscript Curator, who made accessible the Nightingale material in the Mary Adelaide Nutting papers. I would also like to give special thanks to Shirley H. Fondiller and Diana J. Mason, nurse educators and consultants, for their advice and cooperation and for their critical reading of the manuscript. Finally I would like to thank Joe Joseph, a research resource, for making available his private library and its collection of books on English history.

Faithful Friend
The Story of
Florence Nightingale

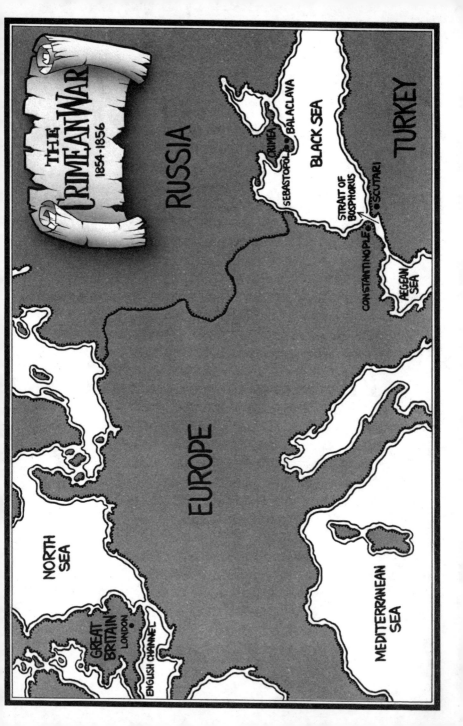

1
A Sister of Charity

The legend started nearly one hundred and fifty years ago in London, England, when on a cold October day in 1854, Florence Nightingale stood on a pier surrounded by thirty-eight nurses. They were ready to board a ship for the long hard voyage to Turkey. The first leg of the journey would take them across the Strait of Dover to Boulogne, France. From there they would travel by coach to Marseilles where they would board another ship. The steamer would sail into the Aegean Sea, up to the Strait of Bosphorus, and drop anchor at Constantinople (now Istanbul).

Nightingale and her nurses were on a special mission to the military hospitals in a small Turkish village called Scutari. There thousands of British soldiers lay wounded and sick in huge barrack hospitals. The dreadful news had reached home that men were dying — not from their battle wounds — but from neglect.

They were the casualties in the Crimean War (1853–1856). Britain had allied herself with France and Turkey to stop the Russian tsar from expanding his empire into Eastern Europe. Such expansion could block Britain's route to her colony, India. Thinking it would be a "little war," the British government sent armies to the battlefronts in 1854. But the Crimean venture would claim tens of thousands of lives before it was over.

The grim facts of soldiers needlessly dying were written up in *The Times*, a London newspaper. The reports by William Howard Russell, the first journalist to report directly from the war front, reached home quickly via a new invention, the electric telegraph. His articles raised public anger to outrage and brought chaos to the War Department.

Russell's dispatches described the acute shortages of medical supplies, drinking water, food, and nursing and medical care. He told how the wounded, on transport ships to the hospitals, begged the few surgeons to help them. In some cases men were kept "for a week without the hand of a medical man coming near their wounds," dying in agony, uncared for and forgotten. Those who finally reached a hospital found that the most basic things were lacking, that there was no linen to make bandages, and that men were dying because the medical staff of the British Army forgot

Thousands of British soldiers died in the Crimean War because of the poor quality of medical care.

that "old rags are necessary for the dressing of wounds."

The whole medical system was shamefully bad, said Russell, with "no dressers and nurses to carry out the surgeons' direction." To drive home his message, he added, "The French are greatly our superiors. . . . They have the help of Sisters of Charity. . . . These devoted women are excellent nurses."

"Why have we no Sisters of Charity?" a reader wrote in a letter to *The Times*.

But England had never employed women nurses in the army. Secretary at War Sidney Herbert, stung by the criticism, decided to try it. He knew where he could find a Sister of Charity. He wrote to Florence Nightingale, a friend of his. On behalf of the government of Great Britain, he asked her to take on the task of selecting female nurses for a mission to the Crimea. "There is but one person in England that I know of who would be capable of organizing and superintending such a scheme," he wrote.

Would she do it? he asked. Would she pick nurses capable of doing hard, serious work? "Would you listen to the request and go and supervise the whole thing?" he asked.

Florence Nightingale had not waited for Sidney Herbert's letter. When the news broke about the lack of nursing care at the war front, she had decided to volunteer her services. She wrote about her plans to Sidney Herbert's wife, Elizabeth, and the two letters crossed each other.

Florence Nightingale was a woman of courage and determination.

Six days after she received Mr. Herbert's letter, Florence Nightingale and her nurses stood on the London pier. In the group were also her friends Selina and Charles Bracebridge, who would be her assistants.

From the moment the announcement was made about the mission, Florence Nightingale became a heroic public figure. People prayed for her and sent contributions for her work. Many, however, questioned her role. A woman to nurse sick and wounded soldiers at the war front? Was a woman fit to take over the work of male orderlies?

And who was Florence Nightingale, everyone asked. A London newspaper, the *Examiner*, head-lined a brief biography with the question, "Who Is Mrs. Nightingale?"

But Florence Nightingale, unconcerned about praise or gossip, stood calmly among her nurses. She was thirty-four years old, tall and slender, un-married, and clearly in command of the situation. She had among her papers the assignment from the War Office outlining her responsibilities. Not outlined but understood was the opportunity to break through prejudice and establish a new fu-ture for women as nurses in the military.

She was ready for the challenge. Without doubt, she knew more about hospital conditions than anyone else in England. People would forget the causes of the Crimean War, but Florence Night-ingale would leave her mark on the world.

How did she arrive at such a peak of influence?

Nothing in her background had pointed in that direction. On the contrary, it was to be a long painful struggle against the values of her upper-class birth to the forlorn filthy hospitals in Scutari. She had to fight to fulfill her vision, and that vision meant being a useful woman in Victorian England.

2
Tutors and Governesses

She was born into a life of wealth, large homes, and travel. Even her name Florence was special. She came into the world while her British parents were in Italy during a three-year honeymoon abroad. They had named their first child Parthenope, the ancient Greek word for Naples, her birthplace. What could be more original than to call the new infant Florence, after the old Tuscan city where she was born on May 12, 1820. Florence? For a girl? Records show that it was the first time a girl was given that name.

The two little sisters were called Flo and Parthe. In their first years they were cradled and cared for by loving Italian nurses. Their parents, Frances and William Edward Nightingale, were enjoying their gay busy lives abroad and were reluctant to return to England. Elegant living and distinguished friends were important to them. For Fanny, as Mrs. Nightingale was called, life meant a continuous whirl of social activity and social success.

Through her mother, Flo could trace her ancestry to a remarkable family. Her great-grandfather Samuel Smith prospered as a merchant, putting together the family fortune. Even when he became rich, he never turned his back on humanitarian causes. His son, William Smith, Flo's grandfather, was a prominent member of the House of Commons for forty years where he too supported liberal causes. Flo was proud of her grandfather's record. He supported the abolition of slavery and was for political rights for religious minorities. The household William Smith and his wife headed had five sons and five daughters, among them Flo's mother, Fanny.

Flo's father, William Edward Nightingale, was also liberal in outlook. Throughout his lifetime he was a Whig, actively supporting Parliamentary reform, and that meant opening up voting rights for the new middle class.

Originally her father's family name was Shore. He changed it to Nightingale when he inherited great wealth from his mother's uncle Peter Nightingale.

Flo's father was striking looking, tall, very thin, and something of a loner. At college he was a friend of Fanny's brother Octavius and often visited the Smith home. He must have been enchanted by the energetic lively family. He was twenty-four and Fanny was thirty when the two decided to get married. It seemed an unlikely match, the beautiful, graceful, extravagant Fanny and the dreamy, lanky, young Nightingale. At first he enjoyed his lively, social wife, but in time he withdrew to the comfort of his books.

Florence was a year old and Parthe two when the family returned to England. After some temporary lodgings, Mr. Nightingale had a home built on the family property in the village of Lea, in Derbyshire, northern England. Lea Hurst, as the house was called, had fifteen bedrooms and stood high atop a knoll, open to the views of the wild moorland country. In the distance were the rolling hills of the countryside. Down a slope in the wood-

Lea Hurst, the Nightingale home, was located in Derbyshire, in northern England.

lands flowed the river Derwent, its lazy sounds reaching Flo's bedroom window. Much as the family loved the beauty of Derbyshire, the large, drafty house was difficult to heat during the bitter cold winter months. Flo remembers a childhood filled with illness, sore throats, and chest colds. She remembered being laid up for a year when she was six.

Not only was the house difficult to heat but Fanny found it too small for her entertaining, and much too far from London and its social events. After much nudging, Mr. Nightingale found a larger home. In 1825, he bought Embley Hall near Romsey in Hampshire, on the border of the New Forest. Here was an estate that made even Mrs. Nightingale happy. The house was surrounded by great natural beauty. Wildflowers covered the meadows and flowering bushes of rhododendron, azalea, and laurel grew along the road leading to the house, making the grounds a showplace spring and summer. Embley would become the family's winter home, close to London and close to friends who made up the Nightingale social circle.

The large Smith family of ten brothers and sisters provided Flo and Parthe with a flood of cousins, a few of whom became intimate friends. When in her teens, Flo could count twenty-seven cousins who kept each other busy in back-and-forth visits. The bright lively Nightingale girls were always popular. Parthe appeared to be the more delicate of the two. Flo, tall and slender, had a special appeal. She had a fine complexion and thick chestnut hair. Even at a young age she appeared serious and had a faraway look in her gray eyes.

Though the social routine was hectic, nothing interfered with the education of the two young girls. Governesses and tutors trained them in music, languages, and dancing. Flo, who always had a great deal on her mind, kept a journal. Tutoring was strict, especially in penmanship. Sara Christie, Flo's governess at the time, made her practice penmanship by writing a moral statement for each letter of the alphabet. "Avoid lying: it leads to every other vice," Flo wrote for the letter A. "Gratitude is the noblest passion of the soul," she said for the letter G. But long before she finished the alphabet she was fed up with the routine, and wrote, "The good of this copy I never could see and I do not like it. . . ." Miss Christie excused her from further moral comments.

Though Flo was extremely fond of Miss Christie, she often found her too strict. When Flo was nine years old she wrote in her journal that Miss Christie made her sit still until she had the "spirit of obedience." As further punishment, she was forbidden to spend time with visiting cousins. Adding to her misery were an eye infection and a bad cold. A few months later her journal entries show a happier mood during a visit to her favorite cousin, Hilary Bonham Carter. That same year she noted that London was dull and that she had spent a month with her Uncle Octavius and Aunt Jane at their country home where Aunt Jane had a party for "poor children."

When Flo was at home, she spent time with her favorite animals. Wandering freely over the Nightingale landscape were dogs, cats, donkeys, ponies, pigs, and other gentle animals. Among them Flo had her special pets, tenderly taking care of a pig or pony when it was sick or injured. At other times, she stayed in her room cataloguing the wildflowers she had picked.

When the girls were ten and eleven years old, Mr. Nightingale interrupted the easy flow of their days. He was not satisfied with their education. Unable to find tutors to meet his high standards, he became their teacher. Flo was delighted with the new arrangement for she adored her father and could now spend a great deal of time with him. He left the teaching of music and drawing to a governess while he undertook to train his daughters in the difficult subjects of Greek, Latin, and mathematics. He also taught them German and Italian history. In their father, Flo and Parthe had a strict and demanding teacher who expected his pupils to do the assignments. Flo often got up at four in the morning to study.

Parthe sometimes found the schoolwork too difficult and escaped to the drawing room to join her mother. But Flo applied herself to the lessons for seven years, learning enough Greek and Latin to translate works from the original into English. She could spend hours conjugating verbs in a for-

Reading and studying were important to young Florence.

eign language. Math fascinated her. One day she would master it so that she would be able to read and formulate tables of statistics.

The discipline of study and the material she was learning made Flo feel alive. She was eager and excited by the world of scholarship outside her door. Her parents noticed that their friends began to enjoy Flo's company, always expressing amazement at how much information she brought to discussions.

3
Tradition

Though life appeared to be rich and exciting, it was, for Flo, only a surface thing. She was not a happy child. She would recall that she was only six when she began to feel different and lonely. There were moments when she was so miserable that she refused to join the family at dinner for fear she would do something monstrous and disgrace herself. What if she used the wrong fork or knife and the family discovered that a strange child lived among them?

Her loneliness and isolation made her stubborn, sullen, and intensely angry at unimportant things. The family could not understand why she was so difficult. "Why does she grumble at troubles which she cannot remedy by grumbling?" her father wrote to her mother when Flo was twelve. Sometimes in her loneliness she sat and watched her favorite birds, the nuthatches, with their black caps and rings around their eyes, run up and down the huge old cypress that grew in front of the Embley house.

How she wished she could be more like her sister, Parthe, who took everything in stride. Parthe enjoyed the social functions that filled the Nightingale life. She loved the continuous flow of visitors, the friends and relatives who made up the social circle, and she enjoyed the constant small talk morning, noon, and night.

All Flo had to do was to relax into the world of material wealth and social manners that surrounded her. She had to be gracious and prepare herself for a life similar to her mother's. And what did mother want? She wanted her two daughters to be shining, well-behaved young women who would make marriages of wealth and position. Was that so bad? For Flo it was. The "world of things and people," as Flo described it in her journal, was empty, trivial. It did not make her feel good. She saw her bright father caught up in an idle life with nothing important to absorb him, and her equally bright mother was busy entertaining.

But Flo yearned for her mother's love, to win her approval, though Fanny Nightingale clearly favored Parthe. For Flo never seemed to do exactly what her mother wanted. There was another reason why she was not smothered in motherly affection. Parents in those days did not understand emotional needs and they did not spend much time with their children. In upper-class society, mothers were concerned with molding their children to play their roles.

Flo was increasingly miserable, and to free herself from her wretched feelings of isolation, she began to escape into a dream world. In daydreaming she could comfort herself, see herself as heroic. She could be a Joan of Arc.

She found another outlet for her loneliness in strong friendships. Early on she attached herself to Sara Christie, her governess. Her best friend was her cousin Hilary Bonham Carter, and she had a crush on her cousin Marianne, a beautiful, unpredictable young woman.

Her favorite person was her gentle sweet Aunt Mai. Aunt Mai, whose maiden name was Mary Shore, was Flo's father's sister and married to her mother's brother, Samuel Smith. From both sides of the family Aunt Mai was related to Flo and deeply sympathetic to her niece's yearnings. Flo became devoted to Aunt Mai's baby son, Shore. She felt at peace when she held him in her arms and when she took care of other children, especially if they were ill. She felt useful when her ailing Grandmother Smith came for a long visit. Flo was attentive, reading to her, visiting with her, holding her hand.

In the villages of Lea and Wellow, where the family homes were located, Flo began to observe another life. She saw the poor who lived in squalid homes and often did not have enough to eat. On her way to London in the family carriage, she rode

The poor people in the villages near Lea Hurst had a great impact on Florence Nightingale's life.

through slum neighborhoods and factory towns, noticing the ragged street children.

Like other wealthy women, Flo began to do charity work, accompanying her mother on her rounds to the cottages in the village, bringing food, clothing, and medicine to the needy. Her parents supported a school in Derbyshire where a single teacher taught the young and the old. Flo sometimes helped at special events. But she had to learn that charity work was only a gesture, that one did not get caught up in it. Nor did Flo ever question why so many were poor and a few so rich.

Tradition and custom dictated the routine of Flo's home. She and her sister were being trained to be dutiful daughters in preparation for being dutiful wives. Only through a good marriage, went the thinking at the time, could a young lady find true happiness and a mission in life. Flo and Parthe had to learn to run a household, manage the servants, entertain, and know how to embroider and sew. They had to learn the skills of dancing, drawing, and music. More than anything, they were schooled in the art of small talk. While men were discussing politics or world events, women were not to bother their heads about such weighty subjects.

Not only was the family shaping Flo into young womanhood, the church and the law also taught her her place. The Nightingales attended services at the Anglican Church of England. The message was clear in the sermons Flo heard: Women must be pious, pure, submissive, and devoted to family. And what did English law say? It said that women could not vote and could not inherit property. Flo knew that neither she nor Parthe nor her mother could inherit her father's estate. Only a male had such a right, so that her father's vast wealth would pass on to the next of kin who had a son. In this case it was Aunt Mai and her son Shore.

Wherever Flo turned she was tied down. What would happen if she got married? Then she would lose the little freedom she had. Her property and income would become the husband's. Even if the husband was brutal, a woman could not sue for divorce, and if she left him, he gained custody of the children.

Mrs. Nightingale with Florence (standing) and Parthe in 1828.

Flo lived in what has been called a "gilded cage." She was oppressed by wealth, not by poverty. She did not have to work in a factory or a coal mine or on the farm. She was asked only to enhance a social setting with brilliant manners.

But she could not stand the sheltered, easy life that made her feel useless. She was lonely and felt cut off and hopeless. She wanted to use her energy and bright mind, to feel the vitality of the world around her. How could she avoid a shallow life and also be an obedient daughter? More and more she escaped into a dream world; and she wrote passionate letters to her friends; and she poured out her heart in her private notes, revealing the demons that obsessed her.

Sister Parthe was no comfort. Like her mother, she enjoyed drawing room society. In a way she seemed to resent Flo's bright searching mind and her leadership. Parthe would have been happy to follow Flo around, but Flo was not interested in such a situation.

In the turmoil of these days, Flo had a strange experience. "On February 7, 1837," she wrote in her journal, "God spoke to me and called me to His service." She was not yet seventeen, and she was sensitive and high strung. In the dream world in which she lived, the voice was real. It comforted her and gave her hope. She was sure that God would direct her further. In a surge of religious feeling, she spent three months working hard among the needy neighbors in the village.

Flo's problems did not stop her mother's plans. She was determined to launch the girls into society at a brilliant social affair. In the absence of a London home, Mrs. Nightingale insisted that Embley Hall had to be enlarged for the occasion. Mr. Nightingale agreed and drew up plans for an addition of six bedrooms, new kitchens, a renovated exterior, and redecorated interior. To avoid the noise and clutter of such major renovations, the Nightingales planned a leisurely trip to Italy and France.

Buoyed up by the call from God, Flo entered fully into the spirit of foreign travel. On September 8, 1837, the family was on its way. Joined by nurse-

Florence and Parthe were raised to be proper society women.

maid Gale and the French maid Thérèse, they took a steam packet from Southampton to Le Havre, France, where their own carriage met them and carried them through France and Italy.

Parthe took along a supply of sketchpads, which she filled with fine sketches of cathedrals and street scenes. Flo, the writer and blossoming statistician, kept a careful record of details. She noted their hour of arrival and departure in each city, its population, and the distance from one to the other. She described her visits to cathedrals and museums, and the beauty of the countryside. But she also noted the large number of beggars on the streets and the widespread poverty of certain neighborhoods.

Though increasingly aware of social conditions, Flo enjoyed the excitement of high society. Her life was a round of opera, concerts, balls, and dances. Opera enchanted her. She was "music mad," she wrote to her cousin Hilary, and she took music lessons in Florence, the city of her birth.

Italy was full of another kind of excitement. People were caught up in the fight for freedom, in struggles to create one nation out of its many states. Flo became interested in political affairs and read books on Italian history. The revolutionary leader Giuseppe Mazzini became one of her heroes. To escape arrest, he had fled into exile along with many of his compatriots. When the Nightingales left Italy for Geneva, Switzerland, they mixed with the Italian exile community. Flo listened to the stories of Italian patriots and their lives in exile. Their dedication inflamed her young mind. It seemed a wonderful way to live, to give one's life for one's country.

From Geneva the family traveled to Paris to take over a luxurious apartment on the Place Vendôme for the winter. Through a letter of introduction, the Nightingales met Mary Clarke, a long-time resident of Paris. The unconventional, vivacious "Clarkey," as she was called, made Paris exciting for Flo and Parthe, introducing them to writers, artists, and politicians. Among them was the scholar Julius Mohl, whom Miss Clarke would later marry.

In this brilliant intellectual circle, Flo was radiant and excited by her social success. To her dismay, she discovered that part of her was eager "to shine in society."

4
The Wider World

Back home in England it looked as if Flo's life would be one of glittering entertainment. The Nightingales spent weeks in London during which Flo and Parthe were presented at court at the Queen's birthday Drawing Room. Flo looked gorgeous in a white gown bought in Paris. Her parents beamed with approval.

The weeks continued on a triumphal swing. Full of excitement, and in the company of cousin Marianne Nicholson, Flo went from party to party, to gallery openings, to the opera, wherever the fashionable gathered. Her pleasure came largely from being with Marianne, whom Flo loved. But the glamorous, gifted Marianne was temperamental, kind and comforting one moment, cruel and indifferent the next. Complicating the relationship was Marianne's brother Henry. He was in love with Flo and proposed marriage. But Flo rejected him, and Marianne, in a fit of anger, broke off their friendship. Flo, whose mood changes could be extreme, went from happiness to despair.

She threw herself into the decorations for the new Embley Hall to which the family returned after the London season. It was now an ornate mansion spreading out amid formal gardens and a long stretch of meadow. Old trees, seasonal flowers, and birds all around made it a showplace. Flo and Parthe helped select fabric for chair covers, and they admired the carpets and wall hangings sent from abroad. To Parthe the new Embley was so beautiful, it was an "Eden or fairy land." Flo too was struck by the "blaze of beauty." To her cousin Hilary, she wrote, "the voice of birds is like the angels calling me with their songs. . . ."

When the excitement was over, there was the old routine. Flo was nineteen and the future looked bleak. Life was empty, filled with trivia. She wanted to be part of the struggles for change taking place outside the gates of Embley Hall. Institutions and tradition were keeping Flo in her place. At the same time there were social and political movements creating upheaval.

The Industrial Revolution in England gave birth to a whole new social order: a large middle class of merchants and businessmen and a working class. Many of the romantic valleys of Derbyshire in the north of England, where Flo lived, had become factory towns for hosiery mills, coal mines, steel and machine shops. Flo was familiar with the deprived homes of workers and the painful sight of ill-fed and hungry children.

Increasingly aware of the world outside, she knew about labor in factories, that men, women, and children worked twelve to fourteen hours a day, that they died young from infectious diseases. The sufferings of thousands in the early 1840s was so terrible that the period was called the "hungry years."

Especially tragic was the use of child labor. Children as young as five and six, and sometimes younger, worked in mines where they were quickly broken down by accidents and crippling diseases. The horrible conditions called to people of con-

Charles Dickens wrote about the horrible working and living conditions of the poor.

science. The poet Elizabeth Barrett Browning described the conditions of child labor in her poem, "The Cry of the Children."

> "For oh," say the children, "we are weary,
>   And we cannot run or leap; . . .
> For, all day, we drag our burden tiring
>   Through the coal-dark underground;
> Or, all day, we drive the wheels of iron
>   In the factories, round and round."

Flo was familiar with other writers who took their stand. She had read the works of Charles Dickens, who described the grim world of the working class in *Hard Times*. His other works, *Oliver Twist* and *Nicholas Nickelby*, also described the cruel world of the poor.

To improve their conditions, workers went out on strike and joined trade unions and other organizations.

The discontent was so widespread that it found its way into the Nightingale drawing room, for even the upper class agreed that something had to be done. Many urged reductions in the price of food; doctors tried to check the spread of disease in the city slums; Lord Shaftesbury, a Nightingale friend, led the fight to reduce working hours of women and children in textile factories.

Flo turned to her Aunt Julia, her mother's unmarried sister. Both she and cousin Hilary adored their Aunt Ju, as they called her. She mixed in enlightened circles, among courageous women re-

Lord Shaftesbury was a leader in the fight to reform factory conditions for women and children.

belling against narrow lives, fighting to gain their rights. Aunt Julia kept her nieces informed. She told them about Lucretia Mott, the American feminist and reformer. In June, 1840, Miss Mott had arrived with the U.S. delegation to London to attend the convention called by the British and Foreign Anti-Slavery Society. She was one of four women in the U.S. delegation of seven. The male English delegates refused to permit the women to speak and participate in discussions. They called their presence "subversive of the principle and tradition of the country, contrary to the word of God." The effect of their decision was electrifying. To give Miss Mott a platform, the women of London

Lucretia Mott was an American feminist and reformer.

arranged a meeting at a Quaker Chapel. In the audience were Aunt Jane and Aunt Julia. Flo and Parthe were not there, but they supported the Quaker meeting.

Within the growing circle of advanced women Flo could have found a shelter but she remained at home, determined to win understanding from her family for her point of view. By the time she was twenty, she was morose, restless, casting about for a way to escape her idle life. Perhaps religion? She thought of converting to Catholicism, but that was not the answer. If only she were a man, she thought, she could be a clergyman and take part in God's work that way. Or she could

31

attend a college and get involved in disciplined study.

Disciplined study finally helped her over her crisis. Aunt Mai was the hero of the occasion, arranging for Flo to study mathematics for which she had expressed a desire. At first the two women started their studies early in the morning. At a later date, when Flo was visiting Aunt Jane, a mathematics master was brought in. During April and May in 1840, she had math lessons twice a week. All this had to be done over the objections of Mrs. Nightingale, who worried that Flo would neglect her home duties. And what did she need math for?

Embley as usual was awhirl with parties. Flo's friend Clarkey was a house guest. Though Flo felt dull and irritable, it was not apparent to the visitors. She was a smashing success, attractive and elegant, impressing everyone with her wit and scholarship. But she was hard on herself, writing in her private notes, "All I do is done to win admiration."

She was twenty-two when she met the poet and writer Richard Monckton Milnes. Milnes, at age thirty-three, was working on a campaign to improve prison treatment of young criminals, insisting on separate housing for them. Milnes fell in love with Flo and visited Embley often. For several years he courted her, and Flo was grateful for his company. In her way she loved him, respected him, and needed him. She longed for a great love to sweep her up, one in which her passionate nature would find fulfillment. Yet when Milnes insisted on an answer to his proposal of marriage, Flo hesitated. She was in conflict and anguish over her answer. In the end she refused him.

Her decision filled her with acute pain. She knew what she was giving up: the golden opportunity to take her place in the married upper-class crowd. And she knew what she had to gain: the possibilities of a career that would be uncluttered by responsibilities to another person. In her private notes she explained her actions. She could not satisfy her own nature, she wrote, "by spending a life with him [Milnes] in making society and arranging domestic things." She had to be the center of her own life, not of someone else's.

Flo's rejection caused a family crisis. The marriage would have been a social highlight for Mrs. Nightingale. To escape from her angry family and from her own pain, Flo found comfort among the villagers of Lea. She went down the hill into the town carrying medicines, blankets, and food. She spent days in the cottages nursing the sick, feeling useful and needed. If she could make nursing her life's work, she would be content. "My soul was at home," she wrote. "I wanted no other heaven," thankful "for the glimpse of what it is to *live*."

5
Marking Time

Her name was Julia Ward Howe. Her husband was Samuel Gridley Howe. For a few days in 1844 they were guests at Embley Hall.

The Howes were Americans, active in the anti-slavery movement. Mrs. Howe was also a supporter of woman suffrage, peace, and social reform. Dr. Howe was famous for his successful schools that taught blind deaf-mutes.

Mrs. Howe, in her *Reminiscences*, recalls meeting Florence Nightingale, describing her as "rather elegant than beautiful; she was tall and graceful of figure, her countenance mobile and expressive, her conversation was interesting."

Flo asked Dr. Howe to meet with her one morning before breakfast. She wanted to discuss with him her choice of work. "If I should determine to study nursing," she said to him, "and to devote my

Julia Ward Howe was the author of The Battle Hymn of the Republic.

life to that profession, do you think it would be a dreadful thing?"

"By no means," Dr. Howe replied. "I think it would be a very good thing."

The idea of *studying* nursing put Flo ahead of her time. She realized that nursing meant more than holding the hand of a sick person, that it required training and knowledge. She had seen a poor woman in town die because the person attending her knew nothing about medications and nursing procedures.

Though her goal was becoming clearer, her despondence remained, as a letter to the Howes reveals. She wrote to them while she was taking care of her grandmother Shore. "I like walking in the valley of the shadow of death as I do here," she wrote. "There is something in the stillness and silence of it which levels all earthly troubles. . . ."

She continued on a round of nursing care, comforting the ailing Mrs. Gale, her nursemaid, holding her hand to the end.

She was all of twenty-five at the end of 1845 when she wrote in her notes, "I am glad to be growing old." But she was a fighter. In her mind she was hatching a bold plan about which she wrote to Hilary: "You must dig for hidden treasure *in silence* or you will not find it," she wrote, "and so I dug after my poor little plan in silence even from you. It was to go to be a nurse at Salisbury Hospital for these few months." In her fantasy, she would return from the nursing experience, take a small house in West Wellow near Embley, and organize a Protestant Sisterhood of Charity. Unlike Catholic Sisterhoods, no one would have to take vows. In this small home, educated women would be able to practice nursing.

She had selected Salisbury because it was only a few miles from Embley, and the head physician, Dr. Fowler, was a friend of the family. Hesitantly, she suggested her plan to her parents. They were outraged. Parthe became hysterical. Her father could not understand why his educated daughter could think of nothing better than to mix with the low characters found in hospitals and nursing. It was as if she had expressed a desire to be a "kitchen maid," Flo would later say.

36

The family's anger was understandable, for nursing in England was a degraded occupation with no health care standards. Scientific principles had yet to be established and nurses were untrained, put to work as much for punishment as a way of earning money. Sanitation and ventilation of sick rooms were unheard of. Beds were often filthy, crammed together to make room for fifty to sixty to a ward. The stench was so overwhelming, patients became sick with nausea.

Flo knew of the reputation of hospitals and nursing, but she did not change her goal. Filthy conditions only meant hard work to turn them around. She did not give up but developed a secret life, studying long medical and health reports in the early morning hours.

Wrapped in a blanket, she pored over British government reports on public health called "Blue Books." She also received material from Clarkey's husband, Mr. Mohl, in Paris. And from Germany she received material that would change her life.

The Baron Bunsen, the Prussian Ambassador to England, had been a guest at Embley. Knowing of Flo's interest in hospitals, he sent her, in 1846, the yearbook of the German Institute of Deaconesses called Kaiserswerth. This Protestant Sisterhood was established by Pastor Theodore Fliedner and his wife Fredericke for the care of the sick poor and discharged prisoners, and for the education of orphans. The deaconesses took no vows, but came voluntarily because they felt a need to do good.

To visit the Institute, to study there, became Flo's ultimate hope. "There my heart is and there, I trust, will one day be my body," she wrote.

After a night of study, she joined the family at breakfast, bright-eyed, innocent, making small talk, her secret hopes shelved for the day. Cheerfully she did her household chores, grateful for something practical to do. "I am fond of housekeeping" and "am fed up to my chin in linen, glass and china," she wrote to Clarkey in December, 1846.

The months dragged on and Flo was again gripped by a feeling of despair. "Oh for some strong thing to sweep this loathsome life into the past," she wrote to Hilary. "I shall never do anything and am worse than dust and nothing. . . ." In religion she found only confirmation of her thoughts, that God's work was in service to the people. The only reason for living, to her way of thinking, was in being useful, in working for the common good.

The family moved around so much, she could not settle into steady work. If she could stay in Lea all year she would be content to work with the poor for the rest of her life. Her sympathies were with them. She and they were the same, she wrote. "We are alike in expecting little from life, much from God; we are taken up with the same objects." Her mind was filled with the miseries of the world. "All the poets sing of the glories of this world appears to me untrue; all the people I see are eaten up with care or poverty or disease."

Florence Nightingale with Charles Bracebridge in the Crimea, based on a sketch by Selina Bracebridge.

And she was eaten up with despair, getting thin and drawn. Travel would divert her, lift her spirits, her parents decided. She would accompany their friends, Selina and Charles Bracebridge, on a trip to Rome in the fall of 1847.

And indeed she spent gloriously happy months in Rome, learning the turn of every street, the sight of every building. She was tireless in a round of museums, galleries, and churches. The Sistine Chapel with the vibrant colors of the Michelangelo frescos became one of the most moving experiences of her life. Looking up at the ceiling was like "looking up into that heaven of angels and prophets," she wrote.

Lord Sidney Herbert was one of Florence's dearest friends and greatest allies.

Through the Bracebridges she met Sidney and Liz Herbert, who would become her devoted friends. Liz Herbert, a beautiful young woman, was kind and generous. Sidney Herbert, a man of thirty-eight, was charming, educated, and very wealthy. Though successful in Parliament, he preferred the quiet life on his large estate, Wilton. Both were devout Christians and dedicated philanthropists. They discussed with Flo their plan to build a hospital for the poor in their village. Though the idea was new, Flo already had definite views on how a hospital should be built and conducted.

Flo was no longer satisfied with only cultural

and social events. She reached out into other aspects of Rome. She made a study of the charitable sisterhoods of the Catholic Church. She went on a retreat for ten days, entering the convent of the Trinità dei Monti, where she observed the special quality of devotion with which nurses did their work. She also studied their methods for the care and teaching of orphans, for she still hoped to start a Protestant Sisterhood in England.

Back home it did not take long for her spirits to sink. There were moments of pleasure in her visits to the Herberts where she met people interested in hospital reform. She impressed everyone with the facts and figures at her fingertips.

When the family was in London, she began to teach at the Ragged Schools. These schools had been started by a cobbler who gathered together poor children and tried to give them some basic care and education. The schools taught a mixture of religion and a simple form of education to the "shoeless, shirtless, and capless children," taking them off the streets.

There were eighty-eight such schools in England when Florence Nightingale became a volunteer teacher. She was devoted to the youngsters, commenting about the former prisoners and other social outcasts, that "those are my brothers and sisters."

But the bits and pieces of volunteer teaching, inspecting hospitals, and studying medical reports did not begin to fill her profound need to give all of herself to improve the staggering misery of the country's poor. Her letters and diaries reveal how morbid she had become. Rarely did a smile cross her face, for nothing made her feel good or happy. In a serious depression, her health again in danger, she began to punish herself, calling herself a hypocrite. She pretended to her friends, she wrote in her notes, to be one sort of person, when in reality her mind and heart were always elsewhere.

6
The Turning Point

She was torn by conflict, unable to break away and unable to settle down. Her family worried over her deteriorating health. Again they urged travel as an escape from her tortured thoughts and suggested that she accompany the Bracebridges on a trip to Egypt and Greece in 1849–1850.

The years of turmoil did not affect Flo's appearance. She was attractive, a slim, graceful woman, her oval face supported by a long slender neck. She wore her thick brown hair parted in the center and combed back giving her a demure look. Under finely etched eyebrows, her large gray eyes were a barometer of her feelings, flashing with wit or, more often, clouded and far away, concealing her inner thoughts.

She looked forward to travel with the Bracebridges. They were twenty years older than she but she felt close to them, especially to Selina of whom she would say, "She was more than a mother to me."

Typical of her need to be thorough, she prepared for her trip up the Nile in disciplined study, making tables of dynasties, copying plans of temples and statues. She also brought along several books on Egyptology. In lyrical letters home she masked a dragging sense of despair, writing about the "glorious golden sun" over everything and "a glassy, breathless lake!"

But she also had an eye for the misery in which many Arabs lived, remarking on slave markets where girls were sold at "£ 2 to £ 9 a head." And she saw that a woman was "nothing but the servant of a man." In Alexandria she took time out from viewing ancient ruins to study the work of the Sisters of Saint Vincent de Paul and their charitable schools of nursing and education.

The side trips became the mainstay of her travels. They consoled her, gave her hope. In Athens, Greece, after viewing the Parthenon, she made her way to an orphanage and school conducted by two American missionaries. Mr. and Mrs. Hill became her friends, answering her countless questions.

The side trips and the beautiful sights were not enough. She felt out of control, on the verge of collapse, as she confessed in her private writings. Nothing distracted her from her single goal. It was obsessive. She had to fulfill herself, to use her intellect and compassion.

Her despair was clear to the Bracebridges. To

help her, they changed their travel plans. Knowing that their decision would not meet with the approval of Flo's parents, they acted on their own responsibility. They decided to return to England via Germany and make a two-week stop at the city of Düsseldorf. Flo would be able to visit Kaiserswerth, the goal of her dreams.

Even on the way there, her spirits lifted. On July 31, 1850, she finally set foot in Kaiserswerth for "a tour of inspection," as her two-week stay was called. She did no nursing but learned in full detail how the place worked. She learned about the organized curriculum, about nurses' uniforms, and about probation or a trial period for applicants. She observed the efforts of the Institute to make nursing an acceptable profession for women.

When she left on August 13, she felt elated, "as if nothing could ever vex me again," she wrote. Her energy renewed, she was able to sit down and write a pamphlet about her experience, directing it to the rich, idle women of England who, like her, were getting sick and going "mad for something to do." She wanted them to know that they could be useful. The pamphlet was printed by the students of the Ragged Colonial School of Westminster, in which she was interested.

For Florence Nightingale, the experience was a turning point. She was moving in a direction she knew was right for her. She was thirty years old, and the answer was clear: to make her life her own.

Strengthening her in her resolve were connections she was making to women who were beginning to transform England. Not only were there Aunt Julia, Aunt Mai, and her cousin Hilary, but she had another cousin, much younger than she, who was making a name in progressive circles. Barbara Leigh Smith was the daughter of her uncle, Fanny's brother Benjamin Smith, an outcast in Fanny's social circle because of his unconventional life-style and radical politics. When Barbara was twenty-one her father made her independent, bestowing on her as on each of his sons and daughters, a yearly income of three hundred pounds. No woman around her, single or married, had such independence. Barbara Smith devoted her life to amending the property laws in the British Isles and succeeded in having a bill passed giving women the legal right to own property.

In that circle of social activists, Florence Nightingale met Elizabeth Blackwell, the first woman to get her medical degree in the United States. Dr. Blackwell, born in Bristol, England, in 1821, had been taken to the United States as a child but often returned to her homeland to visit family and friends. She was in London for further study when she and Florence Nightingale became friends. Dr. Blackwell was naturally sympathetic to Flo's hopes to study nursing and she encouraged her to do so. They met often when Flo was in London, and on occasion Dr. Blackwell visited at Embley Hall.

One such occasion was marked on Dr. Blackwell's memory. She and Flo were outdoors, walk-

Dr. Elizabeth Blackwell was the first woman to receive a medical degree in the United States.

ing around the formal gardens. They had stopped on the lawn in front of the drawing room, and Dr. Blackwell admired the way Embley was built. "Do you know what I always think when I look at that row of windows?" said Flo. "I think how I should turn it into a hospital ward, and just how I would place the beds."

But she was so sensitive, so high strung, that her moods were erratic. One moment she was dizzy with hope; the next she had settled into despair. When she was thirty-one, her morbid thoughts were acute. "I can see nothing but death," she wrote. "My God, what is to become of me?" Her parents, who did not understand what drove her, could no longer deal with her despair and they agreed to let her return to Kaiserswerth for a three-month training period.

In a life of daily drudgery, Flo's will to live returned. She found comfort in the simple surroundings, without a touch of the luxury with which she had been raised. Her small room was located in the Orphan Asylum and she ate her meals with the deaconesses. She found them devoted to their work, pure in heart, and lofty in ideals. To her mother she wrote, "I should be happy here as the day is long if I could hope that I had your smile, your blessing, your sympathy upon it; without which I cannot be quite happy. My beloved people, I cannot bear to grieve you," she wrote. "Trust me, help me," she begged in a passionate letter asserting her need and asking for their approval.

The family remained deaf to her pleas. They were embarrassed by her wish to be a nurse. Their elegant, brilliant Flo working in hospitals among the poor? To them, Kaiserswerth was just an escapade. They made light of her visit and kept it from their circle of friends.

But Flo was increasingly single-minded about the road she had to take. A year later, in 1853, she traveled to Paris with cousin Hilary who hoped to study painting. The two stayed with the Mohls in their home on the Rue du Bac. Flo spent her days methodically inspecting hospitals, infirmaries, and religious institutions. Armed with special permission from French authorities, she observed Paris surgeons at their work. She collected pam-

A nurse from the order of Carmelites.

phlets and reports, planning to write a comparative study of hospital conditions in France and Germany. To receive nurses training, she expected to enter a Sisters of Charity hospital, the Maison de la Providence, when an urgent message called her home. She reached England in time to ease the last days of her ninety-five-year-old grandmother Shore. At the bedside was her father observing his daughter's kindness and gentle ministrations.

Flo had distanced herself from her family. She was ready to break away and had visited Lea Hurst to explain that she was ready to pursue her own life. While there she heard of a job opening that might suit her, that might be a step toward further independence. Though it was not what she wanted, she accepted the offer, agreeing to become superintendent of a London institution called the "Establishment for Gentlewomen during Illness." It was a home run by society men and women for the benefit of sick women of limited income.

Her father, too, took an independent step, settling on Flo a yearly income of five hundred pounds. The generous allowance enabled Flo to take her new position without a salary. Flo returned to Paris to resume her training at the Maison de la Providence. Attached to the premises was a hospital for aged and sick women. Flo, a Protestant, gained admission to the Catholic home through the influence of Bishop Manning, a friend. But she was not permitted to mix with the Sisters, and had to take her meals in her own small room.

Once again she had to cut her stay short. After only two weeks she was struck down with a case of measles. Her convalescence was spent at the Mohls, and when she returned to England, she did not go to Lea Hurst to join her family. She took her own apartment in London. She had left home.

7
Upper Harley Street

She launched her career with complete confidence, as if she had worked before. During negotiations with the committee she was firm about having her own way. She had to be in charge of everything, from selecting new headquarters to choosing the staff. Many on the committee knew her and were sympathetic to her demands. Liz Herbert had joined the group in order to argue Florence Nightingale's cause. But a few questioned whether a society woman like Nightingale could deal with practical matters. Could she really administer a home for the less fortunate? And what would her upper-class parents say about her holding such a position?

But Nightingale was not only confident, she was also somewhat arrogant. She scoffed at committee members who wanted to see a definite plan for the changes she suggested. She asked that they trust her, have faith in her.

The way she handled her first position would cut a pattern for the future. She had to be in control of a situation and have the freedom to apply her skills and knowledge the way she wanted to. Her strong mind and energy made her a compelling force. But she was also realistic and knew how to compromise.

The Harley Street position was in itself a compromise. Working with the poor and neglected had been her goal. That, however, would have caused such a storm of rage at home that the present position was a way of calming her family's fears. They could see something dignified about her present job. In refusing to accept a salary, she put herself into a special category, as if she were performing a public service. And she was, after all, working with society women engaged in charity.

She went into residence on August 21, 1853, in the new location found for the home at Number 1 Upper Harley Street. From the moment she started the job she was busy. In the face of a surge of energy that swept away everything but her work, her despondency and despair vanished. They were things of the past. Within ten days she furnished the new headquarters from top to bottom, getting it ready for the first patients.

She and the committee had a serious difference of opinion over admissions. The committee wanted to maintain the home solely for Protestant women, excluding Catholics and Jews. But Flor-

Florence Nightingale's medicine chest.

ence Nightingale argued that unless she could run a nonsectarian home and admit women of all religions, she would leave the job. She won an agreement on open admissions and also that priests, rabbis, and other spiritual leaders could visit patients. To win that arrangement, she undertook personal responsibility to guarantee that religious leaders would not try to win converts among the other patients.

She was always stretching herself to do more than seemed necessary. But her vision was bold, imaginative, idealistic, giving new shapes to old routines. Within six months she changed the established order and created a well-run establishment.

In quick succession she reduced expenses by overhauling several departments, especially housekeeping. She replaced the chief housekeeper and improved cooking arrangements. She introduced bulk buying, and installed an elevator to bring food to the patients from the kitchen on a lower floor. She suspended a few nurses, checked financial accounts, and installed a new head of surgery. She herself assisted with surgery, and often when something had to be done, she did it herself. On one occasion she suffered a strained back from lifting a patient. She could be found in the basement checking the waste, or in the kitchen poking around.

Busy though she was, she tried to be thoughtful. In a letter to her father she reported the case of a woman who became blind after a failed cataract operation. She was overwhelmed by the tragedy. Patients revealed her kindness in letters, calling her "My good, dear, and faithful Friend," or "My darling Mother."

Harley Street was a satisfying experience. She began the year 1854 "with more feeling of a Happy New Year than ever I had in my life," she wrote. There were disappointments, however. The job was too limited for her abilities and her vision. Her wish to open the home to people of all classes could not be fulfilled, nor could she set up a training school for nurses.

During this period she had her own rooms in London where she saw her friends. In spite of the pressure to live at home, she refused to do so. In a letter to Clarkey she explained that she had thought long and hard on the subject and that it now was an accomplished fact; and she did not wish to discuss it further.

She did return to Lea Hurst for a few days' vacation in August, 1854, when the writer Mrs. Elizabeth Gaskell was a guest. The perceptive Mrs. Gaskell could not make up her mind about what kind of person Florence Nightingale was. She saw her as a woman of cold determination, yet as a gentle and compassionate person whose mission was to serve people. There was a strange elusive quality about her, said Mrs. Gaskell, so that she appeared to be a "creature of another race, so high and angelic. . . . But she seems almost too holy to be talked about as a mere wonder."

Fanny Nightingale, unable to understand the

A bronze cast of Florence Nightingale by Sir John Robert Steele.

strong, strange woman her daughter had become, called her "a wild swan" in a family of ducks.

An outbreak of cholera in London made Florence Nightingale cut short her holiday. She returned to the city to volunteer her services at Middlesex Hospital. She did so knowing that many nurses had died, and that the death rate among patients was very high. For several days she was tireless, admitting women patients, most of whom were considered "outcasts." She undressed them, made them comfortable, and took care of their needs. When the epidemic subsided, she returned to Harley Street.

Word had spread in the medical profession

about her talents and skills. She was considering new job offers, especially one at the newly rebuilt Kings College Hospital where a position was available for training nurses.

Her friends knew that somewhere, somehow, Florence Nightingale would serve the cause of human progress and achieve "undying fame," as her friend the poet Lady Lovelace wrote of her a year earlier in 1852.

8
The Lady-in-Chief

In March, 1854, Britain and France declared war on Tsarist Russia. The battlefront was in the southern part of Russia called the Crimea. By the end of May there were 25,000 British troops and 30,000 French in the army camps on the Black Sea. Many British soldiers, traveling over three thousand miles in cramped transports, arrived sick, suffering from the dread dysentery and cholera.

They were taken to Scutari, on the outskirts of Constantinople, and placed in a hospital lent to the British by the Turks. The hospital, converted from an army barracks, was known for its poor sanitation and limited facilities. Nevertheless, it was filled to overflowing with the sick and wounded from recent battles.

The wounded were still being transported to the

The British hospital in Scutari had filthy conditions and cramped quarters.

hospital when Florence Nightingale and her tired crew of nurses and friends arrived in Constantinople on November 4. Through a heavy dense rain, they were rowed across the narrow Strait of Bosphorus to Scutari. Looming on top of a hill was the Barrack Hospital, a huge quadrangular building made of yellow brick and dominated at each angle by a tower. They climbed the hill and filed up into the northwest tower of the hospital to take over the small rooms that would become their headquarters. Nightingale and Selina Bracebridge shared one room. Mr. Bracebridge and an aide shared another, and the nurses took over similar cramped space. All of them were shocked by the litter and mud in the courtyard and by the filth, vermin, and broken windows everyplace. "I have been well acquainted with the dwellings of the worst part of most of the great cities in Europe," said Florence Nightingale, "but have never been in any atmosphere which I could compare with it [the Barrack Hospital]."

The filth was only part of the hopeless situation. The shortages of equipment and material were astounding, as if the entire British War Office had stopped functioning. In the Barrack Hospital there were not enough beds for the men. There were no medical supplies, drugs, or cloth for bandages. There were no cleansing supplies: no brooms, towels, soap, pails, or mops. Lacking were all kinds of necessities such as spoons, knives, forks, scissors, hot water for laundry, and fuel for cooking. Empty wine and beer bottles served as candlesticks.

The day after Nightingale arrived, more wounded were pouring into the hospital from the battle of Inkerman. Death was all around her. Many died in transport. Others died in surgery, or from dysentery or cholera. And they died quickly, especially the young recruits no more than fifteen years of age. Few soldiers were over thirty.

The high death rate reflected not only gross neglect but also the state of medical care in wartime. Experience was lacking for the proper coordination of medical services, for a single authority who knew what was going on. Not only was this true at the British War Office, but at the hospital itself no one person was in charge of all aspects of the facility. In the early months, for example, no one arranged for ambulances to transport the wounded from the war front to hospitals.

The challenge was there for some bold imaginative person, and it was the challenge Florence Nightingale was ready for. She sailed into the chaos as if she had experience dealing with catastrophes. From the beginning the pressure was intense, but she remained calm, speaking always in a composed gentle voice. She gave the impression that she had studied just such an emergency and knew exactly what to do. In a religious sense, she saw it as the fulfillment of the call from God she

During the Crimean War, Florence Nightingale traveled by carriage between hospitals.

had when she was seventeen, to be a *saviour*.

Instead of being repelled by the filthy hospital conditions, they brought out her rare genius for getting things done. She had to clean up the place. For ten days she did not leave the hospital compound, but drove herself and others in a continuous round of menial tasks. She'd had the foresight to make purchases in Marseilles and had put in a supply of portable stoves and special foods for the sick. Impatient at delays, she made use of funds available to her. These included her own income and money contributed by friends and the public. Additional money was collected by *The Times*, and these funds were in the hands of people sympathetic to her.

At her arrival, she found Mr. McDonald, *The Times* representative, in Scutari. He would be replaced by a benevolent clergyman, Sydney Godolphin Osborne. She sent them along with Mr. Bracebridge to scour the shops in Constantinople for items she needed that were not available from the official Purveyor or supplier at the hospital. She immediately ordered three hundred scrub brushes for cleaning floors and walls. She ordered beds, soap, towels, scissors to cut off men's beards. She quickly removed filthy torn shirts that stuck to men's bodies, and replaced rough canvas sheets and blankets that rubbed against their wounds. She purchased shirts and sheets and blankets and requisitioned special stoves. When supplies were not available locally, she ordered them from London. To feed thousands of men she installed ad-

In addition to reorganizing the hospital, Florence Nightingale spent much of her time caring for the wounded.

ditional kitchens. And to set up a laundry with hot water, she rented a house in Scutari and had it outfitted with boilers.

The tool she used to get the work done was her authority. "She scolds sergeants and orderlies all day long," wrote one of her companions. She herself had become a master of many jobs, writing to her family that "I am really cook, housekeeper, scavenger . . . washerwoman, general dealer, storekeeper."

Nursing soon demanded her full attention. At the beginning soldiers saw her on her knees eight hours a day dressing wounds and comforting patients. Sometimes she was at it twenty hours a day supervising the care of newly arrived wounded. She helped clean them, dress their wounds, feed them, and make them comfortable.

A story is told of her profound compassion. She interceded with surgeons who were forced by shortages in personnel to set aside cases they considered hopeless in order to give their time and energy to those who might survive. Five cases came to Florence Nightingale's attention one day, and she asked permission to care for them. With the help of another nurse, she watched over the wounded men all night, building up their strength with careful feedings. In the morning they were considered strong enough to undergo surgery.

During epidemics of contagious diseases, she disregarded personal danger. In one such epidemic during which three nurses and seven physicians died, she spent hours hovering over men who hung between life and death.

On grounds of propriety she did not permit her nurses in the wards at night. But before she retired, she would make a final tour of the hospital. With a lamp in her hand (thus she became known as "the lady with the lamp"), she walked through the wards, between the endless rows of beds, seeing that each patient was cared for.

She knew that nursing meant "managing the thousand-and-one dry practical details," as she later wrote. It would make the difference between life and death for the wounded and sick. There are things to be done, she said, which "at once separate the true metal from the tinkling brass both among men and women."

To obtain supplies she often defied regulations. Through letters to government officials, she accumulated enough material to become known as the unofficial Purveyor. Orderlies and nurses now came to her supply room in the tower to get food, pots and pans, and sheets.

Actually the nerve center of the hospital was located in the tower where Nightingale lived and kept supplies. In a small living room nearby nurses met with her to discuss the day's work. From that tower she sent her long reports and her list of expenditures to Sidney Herbert. Since she worked without a salary, she would at a later date be reimbursed by the government. From her rooms in the tower, Florence Nightingale controlled everything, using her authority, her resourcefulness, and vision to bring about change. She had become a woman of power.

Not only was she turning the hospital into an efficient facility, she was turning the nurses into an efficient tool. But her strict discipline angered many of them. For their safety she would not permit the nurses to go outside the compound unless accompanied by others. They objected to the dress code. The nurses in the religious orders wore their habits, but for secular nurses Nightingale had devised regulation dress. It consisted of gray tweed wrappers, worsted jackets, caps, a short woolen cape, and a brown scarf bearing in red the legend,

"Scutari Hospital." She was strict about the dress code, forbidding nurses to wear flowers or ribbons on their caps. Most troubling was the exhausting work with few provisions for relaxation, and the rigidity with which Nightingale imposed her will. In letters to families, nurses complained that she was insensitive, demanding blind obedience instead of explaining the regulations.

She had been in Scutari about six weeks when a fresh outbreak of Asiatic cholera brought new hardships and more deaths. In her nightly walks through the wards, she tried to cheer up the critically sick. One seventeen year old was crying out in pain for his mother. Nightingale bent over him

Florence Nightingale acquired the nickname "the lady with the lamp" for her nightly tours of the wards.

and comforted him. The men knew she cared about them. They in turn gave her the energy to carry on her work.

Tragedies mounted as each battle filled the hospital with new cases. By the end of December, the 2,500 beds in the Barrack Hospital were filled, the wounded overflowing into the corridors. Barely eighteen inches of space between beds meant only one person at a time could pass between them. Much more serious was the lack of special rooms for surgery, which now was performed on a patient in full view of others. Those awaiting surgery often refused after seeing the horrors of amputations without an anesthetic. To remedy the situation, Nightingale ordered screens but they could not keep out the cries of agony. "In all our corridors, I think we have not an average of three limbs per man," she said.

To expand the hospital space, she became a construction supervisor. She urged repairs to a burnt-out section of the hospital, and to get the work done properly, she oversaw the work of two hundred construction workers.

9
A New Vision

For six weeks she held every strand of the complex situation in her hand, aware of everything happening, of who was where and who was doing what. Her control was firm when news reached her that another group of forty nurses under the supervision of her friend Mary Stanley would arrive in Scutari. The news stunned her! How had that happened? Who wanted another supervisor of nurses challenging her jurisdiction? She could not face divided responsibility.

The news was more astounding when she learned that her friend Sidney Herbert had organized the new group. Did he want to undermine her authority? But Mr. Herbert had acted only with her welfare in mind. Adding more nurses was his way of relieving the terrible pressure on Florence Nightingale. He did not understand that she would consider it a challenge to her leadership.

Impulsively she thought of resigning, of packing up and going home. But common sense prevailed. Mr. Herbert, learning of her reaction, was full of apologies and suggested that she send the nurses back to England at his expense. She did not take that extreme step, but she did refuse to go down to the pier to greet the new nurses. Instead she sent Mr. Bracebridge to tell Mary Stanley there was no place for her at Scutari.

The situation was finally resolved by the severe wartime conditions. Mary Stanley and her nurses were settled into a new hospital at Koulali, about five miles from the Barrack Hospital. Brutal days of battle flooded Koulali with seriously wounded soldiers and additional nurses were needed. But Mary Stanley herself could not deal with the critical events and she returned to England a few months after her arrival. Within eight months, half her nursing staff was sent home for one shortcoming or another. A few of those who remained were absorbed into the Nightingale contingent.

Nightingale was unable, however, to win the right to be the only supervisor of all nurses, for by the spring of 1855 additional nurses arrived. They were welcomed into the hospitals closer to the war zone in the Crimea itself, making their contribution to improving health standards in military hospitals. No matter how much Florence Nightingale complained, she could not stop religious groups from sending in their Sisters of Charity.

To another volunteer who turned up in Scutari,

As the war raged on, the number of British casualties mounted.

Nightingale gladly handed over the care of the wives and children of the soldiers. She had put some of the women to work in the laundry. But Lady Alicia Blackwood, who had arrived with her missionary husband, found them living in filthy conditions and dressed in rags. Nightingale had neither time nor energy to deal with the group and she welcomed assistance. Lady Blackwood found jobs for many of the women, and also set up a school to teach them and the children how to read and write.

As the winter of 1855 wore on, it brought the cruelty of the Russian weather. British soldiers were not clothed for the bitter cold and mud and snow. In her letters to Sidney Herbert, Nightingale dramatically described the state of the troops as "frost bitten, demi-nude, half-starved, ragged." Men walked into the hospital "barefoot and bare-legged." Her anguish was extreme, trying to figure out how to meet the demands for winter clothing. She not only worried about the whole army but about specific individuals, a Private Jones and a Corporal Smith. On February 5 she wrote to Sidney Herbert, "I do believe that of all those who have been concerned in the fate of the miserable sick, you and I are the only ones who really care for them." Each day brought mounting horrors as fevers and pestilence spread, and she saw the dead carried off to shallow graves in the British military cemetery overlooking the Sea of Marmora.

In reality, Florence Nightingale had become

Florence Nightingale worked with a commission to renovate the unsanitary Barrack Hospital.

more than a supervisor of nurses. She was an administrator and organizer. Growing out of her broad experiences was a changing point of view. A new image was forming in which nursing was part of the entire British Army. She was ready for a mammoth job: to overhaul the military establishment, to reform its hygiene and medical and administrative practices for all time, not just for the Crimean War.

On a daily basis she showed courage, endurance, and a cheerful disposition. But she had a lot of leftover energy. For she had no other interest in life but her work. Into it she put her love and compassion. She transferred her concern for the miserable and hungry people of England to the wounded and sick young men under her care. In her restless mind solutions to problems snapped into place. And because she was determined and persistent, her suggestions were often put into practice.

She advocated the formation of a medical school at Scutari in order to advance "the cause of Medicine and erect it into a Science. . . . There is here no operating room, no dissecting room; post-mortem examinations are seldom made, and . . . no statistics are kept as to between what ages most deaths occur . . ." The only record kept, she complained, was that a "man died on such a day."

As a result of her demands, a Sanitary Commission was appointed in February, 1855. Made up of two medical men, an engineer, and an inspector, the team arrived in Scutari with full responsibility to undertake work and see that it was carried out.

The investigators discovered that the Barrack Hospital was built over a large sewer expelling not only a stench but sewer gas into the wards. The gas accounted in part for the high death rate. The Commission had the sewers and cesspools cleaned out, the walls limewashed, the windows opened up, and the contaminated water purified. The repairs brought a dramatic decline in the death of patients from forty-two percent to twenty-two percent per thousand cases. By the time all the repairs were completed, the Barrack Hospital could boast a death rate of only two percent.

Throughout the first months in Scutari, Nightingale was ably assisted by the Bracebridges, her friends who accompanied her to the Crimea. Selina Bracebridge was her secretarial aide, writing letters and reports, keeping records of purchases and supplies.

Among those who came to help in the spring of 1855 was Alexis Soyer, a chef of the Social Reform Club. In the hungry years of the 1840s in England, he had taught a class for women, including Aunt Julia, on how to make "cheap soup for the hungry poor." During the Irish famine he had also given assistance. Now he came to Scutari at his own expense and took over the kitchen, creating special diets for the very sick and training soldiers how to be cooks.

Though Nightingale made giant strides in many ways, from the beginning she received a mixed welcome by the medical staff. She won some over by her efficiency. Others continued to resent her and made fun of women nurses. An officer, in a letter home, ridiculed the "nightingale." Her idea of nursing made him laugh, he wrote. Some of the ladies were "scrubbing floors." Others referred to her as "the bird." Most men in the military medical establishment could not overcome their prejudice about having women in "a man's world." They were convinced that the military was too rough for women.

But Florence Nightingale succeeded not only because of her own great strength, but because she had the backing of people in power. Sidney Herbert and others in government paid attention to what she had to say. *The Times* of London also supported her, informing the public of her work, building her up as one of the popular heroes of all time. Queen Victoria added to her fame, publicly praising Florence Nightingale. When the Queen sent Christmas gifts of warm scarves to the nurses, she also sent gifts for the soldiers requesting that Nightingale personally distribute them. As if she had been touched with a royal scepter, she now appeared to be an emissary of the Queen, endowed with special power.

A visitor to Scutari at the time described Florence Nightingale as an attractive woman, and though she was not beautiful, her face was not easily forgotten. "She has trained herself to command, and learned the value of conciliation. . . ."

10
"The Heroic Dead"

By April, 1855, the Barrack Hospital was in good order. Beds were only half filled, and many convalescent patients were able to walk around. It seemed a good time to visit the other hospitals across the Black Sea in the Crimea.

On May 2, Florence Nightingale boarded the steamer, the *Robert Lowe*, for the slow sail to the port of Balaclava. With her were Mr. Bracebridge, four nurses, Alexis Soyer, and another cook. Also sailing with her were 420 patients who had recovered from their wounds. They were being returned to the war front "to be shot at again," she wrote to her mother.

In port, the ship became her headquarters, and she was amazed to look out at crowds of spectators trying to get a glimpse of her. She had not realized that she had become famous.

Her plan was to visit two hospitals at Balaclava where female nurses with their own supervisors were at work. The large General Hospital was under the direction of Dr. John Hall. The other, Castle Hospital, was a series of huts built on the hills overlooking the harbor. To get from one to another, she traveled in a cart, or she rode a mare accompanied by men in bright uniforms. What an astonishing sight — Florence Nightingale, an experienced rider, cantering across the hills of southern Crimea to visit hospitals! Soldiers rushed from their tents to greet her and cheer her on, handing her bouquets of wildflowers.

The men cheered her, but she had to come to grips with the one person who had consistently caused trouble: Dr. John Hall, the chief Medical Examiner in the Crimea. Hall was a tough disciplinarian who did not even believe in the use of anesthesia for surgery. Far better, he said, to hear men scream in pain than to have them die silently. From the beginning he was hostile to Nightingale's appointment, seeing it as a challenge to his control. He bluntly declared she had no business coming to the Crimea. Indeed, Nightingale's appointment did confine her to the hospitals in Turkey.

But she was determined to have her way and carefully prepared for her encounter with Dr. Hall. She arranged for the British War Office to approve her visit and for Lord Raglan, Chief of the Army, to be advised about it. She used another bit of strategy. As chief distributor of "Free Gifts," she

Florence Nightingale visited the hospitals, and even the trenches, throughout the Crimea.

had the right to visit all hospitals in the Crimea. She was the one who handed out packages sent to soldiers by their families; and she could use private funds and donations to fill orders for supplies not available through the usual channels.

She visited not only the hospitals but also the trenches. She saw for herself the terrible conditions of men who lived in holes in the ground. Ill fed and ill clothed, they were barely able to survive. In the face of so much hardship, she was impressed with the courage of the common soldier, with his ability to endure.

She also noted that the hospitals were run down and poorly managed, and that the nursing staff did not function well. Though she was careful not to interfere, she nevertheless recommended new huts for the hospitals as well as diet kitchens to be set up by Alexis Soyer.

As usual she seemed tireless, careless about her health, exposing herself to patients with infectious diseases. This time she did not escape the contagion. Weakened from exhaustion, she collapsed. She had caught the Crimean Fever and had to be taken to a hospital. Soldiers carried her on a stretcher from the ship up the slope to Castle Hospital where her best nurse, Mrs. Roberts, took care of her.

For twelve days she lay dangerously ill. In her delirium, feverish thoughts swept through her. At one time she imagined the hospital room was filled with people demanding supplies. At another, she asked for pen and paper to jot down notes. During her illness her hair fell out.

At the news that she was close to death, the troops in Balaclava went into mourning. In Scutari, soldiers wept. "All their trust was in her," a sergeant wrote home. In London, people gathered on the streets exchanging the latest news. At Embley her family felt helpless and offered special prayers at church.

By the end of May Lord Raglan was able to broadcast the news that she was out of danger. Even Queen Victoria expressed her happiness that the "excellent and valuable person Miss Nightingale is safe."

She ignored the advice that she return to England to convalesce. Dr. Hall in particular hoped she would leave so that he could run his hospitals as usual. But her work had changed its course, had grown in dimension. Nothing would convince her to leave the war zone that gave her facts and figures to bolster her demand that conditions for the common soldier must improve.

To calm the clamor that she should rest, she agreed to a temporary stay in a quiet private home overlooking the sea. The four guardsmen who carried her in a litter to her new quarters reported how thin and white-faced she was. Over the weeks her energy returned. In letters to her family she wrote about walking along the shore and seeing the city of Constantinople glowing in the setting sun. She also told them about the cemetery nearby and the gravesites of "the heroic dead," the thousands with whom she identified.

It was to the living, however, that she turned her attention when she recovered. Her compassion for the men in her care kept her courage and energy at a high level. Never did she treat the British soldier as inferior, or as replaceable, or as anyone less than a human being worthy of her best skills. Too many British officers regarded soldiers as "drunken brutes," who were expected to endure hardship and wounds.

But Nightingale had worked with these sons of workers and farmers in the villages near her homes. These were the people she had taught at the Ragged Schools, the ones to whom at the outset she wanted to devote her life. Like social reformers of the period, she believed that people were naturally good. And she had experience with the soldiers in the Crimean War, knew firsthand of their heroism. She admired them for their courage, and she liked them as people. Touched by her concern for them, the men loved her.

On their behalf she was tireless, spending hours in her small office in the barracks tower, wrapped in a wool cloak, writing letters. She wrote to the next of kin of soldiers who had died. Or she took down messages of the dying. Or she wrote letters home dictated to her. In return, family members wrote to her. "I beg to return to you my grateful thanks for all your kindness to my poor dear

Florence Nightingale often wrote down the letters wounded soldiers dictated to their loved ones.

brother and for writing to tell me of his death," a sister wrote. Another said, "I can assure you that you are beloved by every soldier I have seen."

Always creative on the soldiers' behalf, she realized that they went to a canteen because it was the only place for relaxation. In the canteen they always got drunk. To offer an alternative, she organized a coffee house in Scutari, calling it the Inkerman Café. Here soldiers were not encouraged to drink and gamble. To the amazement of those who expected little of the soldiers, they flocked to the café. Using her personal influence further, she reduced drunkenness by exacting promises from the men that they would stop drinking. Many kept their word. "I promised *Her* I would not drink," a soldier would say.

The men spent their paychecks, she discovered, because they did not trust the Paymasters to send their money home. To remedy that situation, Nightingale undertook the job. The government, taking the hint, established special money-order offices in Scutari and other cities. Again, to everyone's amazement, it worked. In six months, 71,000 pounds were sent home.

Her initiative led to the opening of schools and reading rooms for the men. Through supplies sent by her sister and friends, she stacked the rooms with notebooks, illustrated texts, maps, music, plays, and games. The men themselves organized theater and singing groups.

In a letter to her sister, Nightingale expressed her thoughts on the subject. "I have never seen so

teachable and helpful a class as the Army gener-
ally," she wrote. "Give them opportunity . . . to
send money home and they will use it. Give them
schools and lectures and they will come to them.
Give them books and games and amusements and
they will leave off drinking."

The allied victory at Sebastopol in September,
1855, ended the long siege of that beleaguered city.
The battle had filled hospitals and cemeteries. A
month later, in October, Florence Nightingale
again went to the Crimea. She would make a third
visit in the spring of 1856. By then her authority
had been fully established. A directive from the
War Office declared her to be the Superintendent
of the Female Nursing Establishment of the military hospitals of the Army. It meant she could
work in any hospital, but always under medical
supervision. She was still under Dr. Hall's jurisdiction, but he could no longer undermine her
work. And she used her energy in the Crimean
visits to upgrade the hospitals, improving sanitation and nutrition.

The Bracebridges, her able assistants, had returned to London in July, 1855. To help her, her
aunt Mai, Mrs. Smith, arrived in September,
shocked to see how pale and worn her niece had
become. Like Selina Bracebridge, Aunt Mai became a secretary, handling reports, letters, and
records. Grateful for her help, Nightingale said of
her aunt, "There is no one who lifts me up" as she
does.

While she continued her long hours of work,

trying to overhaul medical standards, Nightingale was becoming a legend at home. During her illness people had panicked, and only word of her recovery made them jubilant. They watched for daily reports of her health with the same anxiety they showed for major battles. The Queen too had requested bulletins.

Nightingale's praise had been sung by soldiers writing home to families. Now they were returning to their villages and cities, spreading anecdotes far and wide about their beloved Florence Nightingale. Biographies were written, and verse and poems, among them H.W. Longfellow's poem, "Santa Filomena." She was celebrated in music, in plays, and in portraits. Her likeness adorned china and woodcuts. Thousands of newborn babies were named Florence, as were ships, streets, and even a racehorse!

She was England's great hero. To give the public an opportunity to express their feelings, a meeting was called in London. A wildly enthusiastic overflow crowd listened to speeches by public officials and by a soldier recently returned from the battlefield. Similar meetings were held throughout the country. Out of them came a public collection of 45,000 pounds (about 200,000 dollars) that would make up the Nightingale Fund. The monies were earmarked for her use.

To add to her expression of esteem, the Queen sent Florence Nightingale a jewelled brooch designed by her husband, Prince Albert. It was in the form of a Saint George cross in red enamel,

Queen Victoria honored Florence Nightingale with a jewelled brooch designed by her husband, Prince Albert.

encrusted with diamonds and the Queen's initials. The pin carried the legend, "Blessed are the Merciful," and the word, "Crimea."

Florence Nightingale wore the brooch to the 1855 Christmas dinner at the British Embassy. Another guest, Lady Hornby, in her memoirs of the Crimean War, left a description of the event.

Lady Hornby thought at first that the woman who entered the drawing room was a nun in her "black dress and close cap." Then she realized it was Florence Nightingale, "the greatest of all now in name and honour among women." Lady Hornby was overwhelmed with sadness at Nightingale's "wasted figure and the short brown hair combed over her forehead like a child's." The only ornament on the black dress was a large enameled brooch. "She is very slight, rather above the middle height; her face is long and thin, but this may be from a recent illness and great fatigue. . . . She looks a quiet, persevering, orderly, lady-like woman," she wrote. She described Nightingale in detail, said Lady Hornby, because there must be "a hum all over the world about this celebrated lady."

While they were celebrating her, Nightingale continued to work. Her spirit was indestructible. She had carved out the British Army as her territory and made a study of soldiers in the trenches and in the hospitals. She knew how they spent their leisure and how they spent their money. Into her work she put her passion and vitality. She stayed on through the signing of the peace treaty in March, 1856. She was there after the troops left for home at the end of April. Only when the last hospitals in Balaclava were closed down, was she ready to leave.

Eight thousand British soldiers lay buried in a huge military cemetery. Many died, not from their wounds, but from neglect, unsanitary conditions, red tape, and inefficiency. Nightingale had to make sure that such a disaster never again happened.

Back home, a jubilant public was planning parades, receptions, and balls to honor her upon her return. But she could not face such demonstrations of affection.

11
"I Fight Their Cause"

She declined the offer of a battleship to take her home. And determined to avoid the celebrations awaiting her, she traveled under the name of Miss Smith. Her aunt Mai, who was with her, was Mrs. Smith. Accompanying them was a Queen's messenger to take care of baggage and passports.

At the end of July, 1856, they left Constantinople for Marseilles and Paris. Aunt Mai went on to England while Nightingale stayed on to visit friends. A few days later, she sailed alone for England. From London she took a train to the village Lea, and climbed up the slope to the gabled house on top of the hill. She walked into the arms of her family on August 7, 1856. She was thirty-six years old.

She had gone to the Crimea with her parents'

consent. They were proud to have a daughter who had been called on to serve her country, and the first woman appointed to a leading position. She had gone "at the risk of her very life," the *Examiner* had reported in hailing her. The Nightingales' homes had become depots for hundreds of letters from admirers, letters carefully answered by Parthe. Everywhere people were celebrating the great hero, Florence Nightingale.

Now back with her family, she saw that they looked the same. But they saw that she had aged, that she was thin, pale, and worn. Not even the excitement of being home could wipe the sadness from her face. Years of hard work and tragedy had marked it.

The family urged her to settle down, to rest, eat, and regain her strength. Even her influential friends, seeing her pallor and fatigue, urged her to rest. But she was driven, pointed only in one direction, kept awake at night with ideas and plans. Statistics churned in her head: the sixty percent death rate in the Crimea during the first months of the war; the thousands who had needlessly died. She had changed those figures. But the lessons had to be forced on the government so that such disasters never again occurred. In August, 1856, she dramatically wrote in her private notes, "I stand at the altar of the murdered men, and, while I live, I fight their cause."

An unexpected opportunity would advance her work. The physician to the Queen, Sir James Clark, invited her to his home Birk Hall in the Scottish Highlands. He wrote, he explained, at the Queen's request.

Accompanied by her father, Nightingale traveled to Birk Hall, and on September 21 had her first meeting with Queen Victoria and the Prince Consort. In a two-hour talk, she clarified for them the medical problems in the armed forces and her recommendations for change. Impressed with Florence Nightingale's grasp of the situation, the Queen remarked, "I wish we had her at the War Office." The Prince Consort wrote in his diary: "She put before us all the defects of our present military hospital system, and the reforms that are needed. We are much pleased with her; she is extremely modest."

Royal goodwill was important. The crown could use its power to influence the government in office and help win approval for Nightingale's recommendations. She wanted the appointment of a Royal Commission with the power to review the entire Army Medical Department and the health of the army at home and abroad.

Launched on her work and eager to avoid friction at home, she took rooms at the Burlington Hotel in London. Her old friend and ally Sidney Herbert became the intermediary through whom she reached other men in political office. Though she carefully worked out every detail for the Royal Commission, its actual formation was delayed week after week.

A photograph of Queen Victoria taken in 1866.

The delay played on her nerves and increased her tensions. Obsessed, she drove herself mercilessly, pacing the floors of her rooms at night, neglecting to eat. Her popularity was at its peak, and she must strike while the public was on her side. Memories nagged at her. Writing in her private notes in February, 1857, she expressed her despair. "No one can feel for the Army as I do," she wrote. "These people who talk to us have all fed their children on the fat of the land and dressed them in velvet and silk, while we have been away. I have had to see my children dressed in a dirty blanket and an old pair of regimental trousers, and to see them fed on raw salt meat, and nine thousand of my children are lying, from causes which might have been prevented, in their forgotten graves. But I can never forget. People must have seen that long, long dreadful winter to know what it was."

Nothing stopped her from her work, not rain, fog, or cold. She hurried from one government office to another using the public horse-drawn bus when a private cab was not available.

Finally she won a great victory. The government announced the appointment of a Royal Commission on the Health of the Army and four subcommissions. Because she was a woman she was not appointed to any of the committees, but she exerted her influence through Sidney Herbert, who was named the Commission's chairman. Her sitting room at the Burlington Hotel was so busy with meetings and visitors, it was called the "little war office."

Out of her work and experience came a landmark book, a huge volume called *Notes on Matters Affecting the Health, Efficiency, and Hospital Administration of the British Army.* She used statistics, a new tool in those days, to explore social conditions. In the wide range of subjects, she wrote about the need for sanitary science and dietary kitchens, and the need for administrative changes and new hospital construction. Her studies made her the single great authority on health reform, a consultant to everyone seeking change.

But she was straining her exhausted body to its limit. Friends who urged her to rest were rebuffed, for she had decided that only she held the key to the future and that only her zeal could guarantee an end to the evils she had seen.

At one low point when she felt near death, she drew up her will. Everything went to the army. The funds were to be used to build model barracks and model houses for the married men. Her health continued to deteriorate and in August, 1857, a year after her return from the Crimea, she collapsed. Her mother and Parthe wanted to take care of her, but she turned down their offer. She had to run from the family friction and went to the village of Malvern, known for its rest cures. Her father's visits pleased her for she felt close to him. When he saw how frail she had become, he called on Aunt Mai to nurse her.

When she returned to her rooms at the Burlington Hotel, she started her life as an invalid, a condition Florence Nightingale would be in for the next forty years. For a while, Aunt Mai or cousin Hilary stayed with her to manage the household and act as her social secretary. When they had to move on, an uncle or another cousin would take on the role.

The invalided Florence Nightingale suffered from complete exhaustion rather than from a life-threatening disease. Every nerve and organ had been strained to its limit. Doctors predicted that her health would never improve much, but that good care and rest would prolong her life.

For two years she barely left her bedroom. But in illness as in health, Florence Nightingale was a formidable force. Though she sometimes fainted at the end of a meeting, and she limited her visitors to politically important people, nothing slowed her work. "I believe it is work which keeps both of us alive," her friend Harriet Martineau, also an invalid, remarked.

A litter would rush her off to Malvern when her health was dangerously low. Then she was again back in her rooms writing, thinking, restless to get her thoughts down in working order.

In those same months that she was obsessed with reforming medical care in the British Army, she undertook another gigantic project: to reform health care for the British Army in India. Encouraging her was not only Sidney Herbert but also Lord Stanley, Secretary of State for India.

Her unique experience went into the Report of the Indian Sanitary Commission and its publication of two huge volumes called Blue Books. These books gave a complete picture of native life and the effects of the occupying British forces. Few people read the heavy volumes but many did read a twenty-three-page summary called "Observations by Miss Nightingale." The Observations, illustrated with woodcuts and printed separately, was known as "the little red book." It was closely studied and helped launch the sanitary crusade in India, for Nightingale criticized barrack life, the filthy bazaars, the contaminated water, the lack of ventilation, poor diet, and overcrowding in hospitals as causes for rampant disease and early death in the Indian army.

Her influence skyrocketed, especially after the publication of her book, *Notes on Hospitals*, in 1858. She traced the causes of the high death rate in hospitals to overcrowding, lack of air and light, lack of sanitation, and poor kitchen and laundry facilities.

Health officials and heads of governments asked her advice. The King of Portugal accepted her plans for the construction of a children's hospital. In the United States at the outbreak of the Civil War in 1861, the government consulted her about organizing hospitals for the soldiers. As a result, a Sanitary Commission was formed and women nurses entered hospitals reproducing much of Nightingale's work.

Throughout the late fifties and sixties, she was the woman in the news. Her books were best-

Mothers and children in the English slums lived in poverty.

sellers, especially the 1859 publication of *Notes on Nursing: What It Is and What It Is Not*. She directed the book to the average woman, the one who has to take care of others. Nursing was an art, a profession, she said, not a temporary job that anyone could perform. "A nurse must be something more than a lift or a broom," she wrote. Again she repeated the need for pure water, quiet, ventilation, and beautiful surroundings. Form, color, and light not only raise up the spirits, but also affect the body and aid in recovery, she advised.

A less expensive edition of the book reached factory workers, farmers, and small village residents. Chapters on "Nursing the Well Before They Become Sick" and "Minding Baby" made her name a household word. "You must take care that baby is not startled by loud sudden noises," she cautioned, especially if a baby is asleep. Translations of her book into German, French, and other languages, and editions in the United States, made her popular worldwide.

She was so single-minded, so wrapped up in her work, that she could hardly see what was happening to people around her. Such was the case with her dear friend Sidney Herbert. She refused to see how sick he had become, forcing him to carry through the work he had undertaken. After he died in 1861, she would realize that she was "hard on him." But she desperately needed him to win the fight in government for the reforms they both regarded as essential. His death would be a permanent loss. For five years they had worked together as a team. He was the political figure, the man in government; she was the force behind the scenes. They had brought about lasting changes in army life.

12
The Nightingale School

From her invalid's bed, Florence Nightingale began to address the use of the 45,000 pounds collected during the Crimean War. Uppermost in her mind was the need to establish a training school for nurses.

Why a training school for nurses? Clearly Florence Nightingale did not invent nursing, but she had a different vision of what it should be. She wanted to take it out of the field of menial labor and put it into the field of medicine. In doing so, she was moving with the age in which she lived, an age of social reform and medical progress. In the news was Joseph Lister, who had founded modern antiseptic surgery, dramatically reducing the postoperative death rate. Other medical scientists found new approaches to the diagnosis and cure of the sick. Though Nightingale was not a scientist by training, she nevertheless identified with the trend, especially with the deepening interest in sanitary science.

Science was urging her on, as well as her interest in giving women meaningful employment. The time had come for women to face the reality of working. And she would provide them with training, a career, and a salary so that they could be independent. They would no longer be able to say that they did not know how to do anything.

Her religious convictions gave Nightingale further motive. Since God acted through people, as she had concluded, nursing would be a way to do God's duty. Religious faith would give nurses the strength to face the tragic losses and painful scenes that were part of their work.

The formation of a nurses training school became a scientific experiment. Nightingale knew exactly what she needed to set her experiment into motion.

She chose St. Thomas's Hospital near London Bridge as the site for her school. The large, well-managed facility would have additional space with the construction of a new building. At St. Thomas's she found Mrs. Wardroper, a widow who had raised four children, knew the value of independence and discipline, and was devoted to her work. She could be strict, but she was also charming and flexible, making her exactly the sort of person Miss Nightingale wanted to become superintendent of nurses.

Determined to produce a new type of nurse, she

THE NIGHTINGALE PLEDGE

I SOLEMNLY PLEDGE

myself before God and in the presence of this assembly to pass my life in purity and to practice my profession faithfully. I will abstain from whatever is deleterious and mischievous and will not take or knowingly administer any harmful drug.

I WILL DO ALL IN MY POWER

to elevate the standard of my profession, and will hold in confidence all personal matters committed to my keeping, and all family affairs coming to my knowledge in the practice of my calling.

WITH LOYALTY

will I aid the physician in his work, and devote myself to the welfare of those committed to my care.

Composed in honor of Florence Nightingale, this pledge was first used in 1893 in Detroit, Michigan.

opened the doors of the school to women of every class and religion. She looked for people who were intelligent, idealistic, and trainable. Her comments about the applicants she interviewed were sharp and incisive, often showing her upper-class bias. She wrote about one applicant, "Flippant, pretension-y, veil down, ambitious, clever . . ." About another, "A good little thing, spirited," and about another, "Seems a woman of good feeling and bad sense."

Fifteen women, called probationers, started their training in June, 1860, when the Nightingale School for Nurses opened its doors. They became Nightingale's personal charges. To mold the newcomers to fit her vision, she oversaw every aspect of their daily lives and training. The Fund paid them a stipend and expenses for lodging and laundry. Nightingale selected their uniforms: brown dresses over which they wore bright white collars, aprons, and caps. She arranged their living quarters, a bedroom for each probationer, and a communal sitting room decorated with books, flowers, and pictures. The invalided Nightingale did all the work from her home through friends who became her messengers.

At the end of the work day, when the exhausted "probies" wanted to rush off to bed, they still had one chore. They had to write up the day's work. Through these reports and Mrs. Wardroper's confidential notes, Florence Nightingale kept the young students under close scrutiny.

Many resented the strict discipline, the supervision of their days and nights. But Florence Nightingale knew exactly what she was doing. In establishing nursing as a profession, she had to change the rules and create a new type of woman who could function in this new sphere of work. In a long view, she saw the first graduates as pioneers who would carry her message throughout the world. That message meant high standards of health care for people of all classes and religions.

Between 1860, when the school opened, and 1903, some two thousand nurses received certificates from the Nightingale School. Though the

Florence Nightingale looks out of the window at nurses from her school in 1887.

number was small, their influence was great, for many became superintendents of hospitals or other large institutions in Europe, or in the British colonies, or in the United States. Wherever they were, they established the principles of the Nightingale School for Nurses.

Through her work, women gained a new level of power. To start with, she had taken the supervision of nursing out of a man's hands and given it to a woman. She also insisted that women were to be paid wages. Nursing was no longer a voluntary service in which women were regarded as maids or companions. Firm as she was about these points, she was equally so about another, a personal prejudice. She limited nursing to unmarried or widowed women. Head nurses who married had to resign. For Florence Nightingale work was a substitute for marriage.

Over the years, she had moved around from one rented house to another. In October, 1865, she finally settled into her own home on 10 South Street, in the Mayfair section of London. The house was a gift from her father.

Though called a small house, it had four floors, an attic, and a basement. The place was cluttered with bookcases filled with Blue Books (government reports) and cartons of her papers and letters. Reflecting her health habits, the windows of her bedroom were open to light and sun. Fresh flowers, photographs, and paintings were everywhere. Here, settled into a sofa or lounge, a shawl draped over her head and shoulders, she did her work. Or she entertained visitors who came by appointment.

Her illnesses were often painful. She was afflicted with a heart condition and a severe form of rheumatism. Sometimes the pain was so intense, her position could not be changed for forty-eight hours. At such times she took medication to relieve the pain.

On the surface she remained softspoken and calm, but her thoughts were relentless and gave her no rest. Her invalidism served a purpose, freeing her from social obligations. She could use her time to do the work she considered urgent. In a way she lived in her own world filled with her own vision. She controlled that world and as its master she was sharp and clever. Among her weapons was the written word. She was a nonstop writer, producing letters, reports, and notes that carried her messages far and wide. Letters to friends were different for they were outlets for her anger and her moods.

In many ways she was a woman of contradictions. Though interested in improving health conditions for the common people, she never allied herself with mass movements of workers fighting for change or even with the women's movement. Rather she used her upper-class origin, working through influential men in government, many of whom were personal friends. She demanded their time as if they had no other lives to lead.

But what a beacon of light she had become! Her knowledge and experience were sought world-wide. Requests for advice poured into her South Street home. As a result, she used her experience to help solve health problems in local communities as well as in foreign countries.

13
"Trumpet Calls to Duty"

To reach out into communities, Nightingale set up a special program for midwives. Money from the Nightingale Fund was used for a six-month training program at King's College Hospital. The women were then to return to their villages to put into practice the new methods they had learned.

She intervened in maternity hospitals when she learned that more women were dying after giving birth in hospitals than at home. After collecting facts and figures, she launched an experiment under careful sanitary conditions. The results confirmed her analysis about the need for "incessant cleanliness and ventilation."

Work on behalf of the poor always won her attention. When William Rathbone, a wealthy merchant and shipowner in Liverpool, asked for her help, she readily gave it. Rathbone was one of those rare figures dear to Miss Nightingale, an authentic philanthropist deeply involved in improving the miserable conditions in the Liverpool slums. She would call him "one of God's best and greatest sons."

When he wrote to Florence Nightingale that he could not find reliable nurses, she found time to help him. Acting on her suggestion, he established a Training School and Home for Nurses, which turned out to be a huge success. Like so many others with whom she worked, Rathbone became devoted to her and until his death, he kept her house filled with flowering plants.

Helping Mr. Rathbone find a ready supply of trained nurses did not end her work with him. He was already looking into conditions in the Liverpool workhouse, a terror-filled facility for the poor sick. As many as 1,200 people were crowded into a small space. Their bedding was changed once a month, their shirts every seven weeks, and their food was so paltry, many died from starvation. The nurses taking care of the sick were paupers themselves, untrained, and often drunk. "It is Scutari over again," Nightingale commented.

Using the Liverpool workhouse as an experiment, she sent in twelve trained nurses with Agnes Jones as the able and dedicated superior. It took three years before Miss Jones brought the facility into the new age, making it a model for others.

From the Liverpool experience, Miss Nightingale began to see the whole picture in the care of the sick poor. Changes had to be made at every level, she said, including the heads of the Poor Law Board, who had outdated notions.

The sick poor were not to be regarded as paupers with no future, but as people to be nursed back to health, she said. They needed their own establishments and proper care. To her way of thinking, a sick person had a special claim and was above any classification except to be cured.

She had found appalling conditions in which children lived in the same facility with the insane. The sick, the insane, the incurable, and children should not be lumped together. In an article called "A Note on Pauperism," published in March, 1869,

A street in London in 1870.

she made her thoughts known. The sick and the incapable should be removed from the work-house; pauper children should be boarded out and educated at industrial schools; the State should take care of housing for the poor. The hungry, she said, should not be punished for being hungry. They should be taught to feed themselves.

Her crusade to improve public health won her great support. Backing her was *The Times* of London and a medical magazine, *Lancet*. Her efforts helped launch a Work-House Reform Movement which led to legislation on behalf of the poor.

Nursing and the use of trained nurses remained the central core of everything Florence Nightingale did. She made the point over and over that only those trained in the latest scientific methods could bring about a higher standard of health care.

Among those inspired by her work was a Swiss doctor, Henri Dunant. He formed a volunteer aid society in 1864 and called it the Red Cross, acknowledging Florence Nightingale as his inspiration. Growing out of the Red Cross was the idea that wounded soldiers should be considered "neutral" regardless of which side of the war they were on. In 1867, the Conference of Red Cross Societies in Paris awarded her a gold medal. When the British branch was formed in 1870, Nightingale became their consultant. In a letter to the new organization she repeated her caution that nursing was not for "sentimental enthusiasts," but for "lovers of hard work."

From 1872 on she began writing an anniversary

address to the probationers, always reminding them of their special calling. Not until 1882 did she personally pay a visit to St. Thomas's Hospital. It was an historic occasion, throwing everyone at the hospital into a frenzy. What if the lady disapproved of the way the school looked! She had, after all, designed it from her invalid's couch, and arranged every detail without actually seeing it.

In her address on that occasion, she urged them to make progress, to keep up with medical advances, and to continue their education. "Unless," she said, "we are making *progress* every year, every month, every week . . . we are going back." Her talk was known as "trumpet calls to duty."

14
The Legend

After ten years of being housebound, she ventured out to visit her family at Embley. Her mother, now seventy-eight years old, had been shaken up in a carriage accident, and Flo, as the family still called her, came to take care of her. She found her mother in a "delapidated" state and much "gentler, calmer, more thoughtful," she wrote to Clarkey. In other visits to Embley and Lea Hurst, daughter and mother drew closer together and often discussed the past. Mrs. Nightingale blamed herself for much of the misunderstandings and admitted, "You would have done nothing in life, if you had not resisted me."

The 1870s found Nightingale in low spirits, caused partly by the political situation. The men in office were not sympathetic to her cause and

Florence Nightingale in 1859.

she felt isolated, as if she had accomplished nothing. To make matters worse, the War Office no longer called on her for advice. She wrote in her notes about her loneliness, berating herself for her lack of patience.

Her loneliness deepened with the sudden death of her father in 1874. In the same period, Charles and Selina Bracebridge died. She thought of these friends who had shared her experiences in Scutari, as "the creators of my life."

She occupied herself with settling her father's estate. The two houses and vast land holdings passed on to Aunt Mai and her son, Shore. Her mother, no longer the owner of Embley and Lea Hurst, went to live with Shore and his family in London.

Religion sustained her throughout her life. She always found solace in God, believing that one served Him when one served people.

Despondent or not, Nightingale's mind was restless and creative. She reassessed her views about India after a terrible famine in which hundreds of thousands of children died. What was the point, she wanted to know, of trying to keep people healthy if you could not keep them alive. What India needed, she concluded, was a good system of irrigation, education, and land reform.

Victorian England was not standing still. Each decade added a list of improvements in the conditions of workers and women. Huge working-class demonstrations brought about voting rights. Women's groups won better divorce laws, opportunities for higher education, and other changes.

In 1886, when Florence Nightingale was ready to withdraw completely from public life, she became involved in a controversy that would last seven years. It was called the "Nurses Battle." On one side was Nightingale. On the other was Ethel Bedford-Fenwick, leading the British Nurses Association. Bedford-Fenwick was a formidable opponent who had the support of the Queen's daughter, Princess Christian.

The battle centered on whether or not to establish a General Register of Nurses. Supporters wanted to provide qualified nurses with credentials that would make it easier for them to get jobs

Florence Nightingale in her bedroom at 10 South Street.

through a central registry that would have on file all the data about nurses. Nightingale, on the other hand, argued that such a system would lower standards, that only the most recent character references could establish an applicant's loyalty, devotion, and hard work.

Arguments were bitter, flooded with petitions, pamphlets, and meetings. When it was over, a charter was granted to the Nurses Association, but in such a weakened form that it was not effective. Nightingale appeared to win that fight, but soon after her death a central registry was put into effect.

Nightingale had a continuous outpouring of fresh insights. This was clear in a paper of hers read at the World's Columbian Exposition in Chicago in 1893. Titled "Sick Nursing and Health Nursing," she called for "Health Missioners" to visit families to teach them how to stay well. Her ideas can be seen at work in today's community and public health systems.

Moving into her late years, she mourned her mother's death in 1880. Ten years later her sister Parthe died. The two had become closer. "Her love for you was intense," Parthe's husband, Lord Verney, wrote to Florence Nightingale. The Verney estate at Claydon became Nightingale's country home where she spent time with her brother-in-law. When she was seventy-five, she could say, "Life is a splendid gift!" She was deep in correspondence with nurses and matrons and still saw important visitors concerned with health care.

Much as she valued public support, she remained shy of public acclaim. Only reluctantly did she agree to contribute memorabilia to the Queen's Diamond Jubilee Celebration in 1897. At Embley the carriage was found that she used in the Crimea to travel between hospitals. Her lamp too was exhibited. After much pressure, she permitted the display of a bust and portrait.

At eighty she was forced back into complete invalidism. Again she never left her home. At first she lost her eyesight, putting an end to her reading and writing. A nurse stayed with her. Her house on South Street was a showplace of bright sunshine and the vivid colors of plants and flowers.

Queen Victoria's Diamond Jubilee procession in 1897.

Running freely around were her Persian kittens. She was following her own advice that pets make good companions for the sick.

In her final decade she was visited by a new generation of nieces, nephews, and cousins with whom she had kept up a lively correspondence. To one niece who had become a vegetarian, she wrote, "I send you some Egyptian lentils. I have them every night for supper, done in milk."

Close friends were dying, but her spirits were unflagging, and she could finally say, "There is much to live for. I have lost much in failures and disappointments, as well as in grief, but do you know, life is more precious to me in my old age."

She was celebrated all over the world as a great woman. On her birthdays school children sent letters, and Crimean War veterans sent flowers. In 1907, King Edward, who followed Queen Victoria to the throne, bestowed on her the Order of Merit, the first woman to receive the honor. The following year she became the first woman to receive the Freedom of the City of London.

As she approached her ninetieth birthday, her mind wandered. She was hardly aware of what was going on around her. A portrait at the time shows her as a heavyset woman with a rounded face. A white lace shawl over her gray hair is tied under her chin.

At age ninety and three months, on August 13, 1910, Florence Nightingale died in her sleep. To the end she refused public honors, declining the proposal of a national funeral and burial in West-

*American war nurses paying their respects at Florence
Nightingale's tomb in Romsey.*

minster Abbey. Carrying out her wishes, she was buried in a simple ceremony in her home village of Romsey near Embley Hall. Flowers covered the churchyard, and crowds of people — women, men, and children — filled the grounds to watch six Sergeants of the Guards carry her coffin to the family grave, placing it beside her father and mother. On her tombstone was the simple inscription:

F.N. born 1820. Died 1910.

Bibliography

Writings by Florence Nightingale:

Cassandra. New York: Feminist Press at the City University of New York, 1979.

Florence Nightingale to Her Nurses: A Selection from Miss Nightingale's Addresses to Probationers and Nurses of the Nightingale School at St. Thomas's Hospital. London: Macmillan, 1914.

Health Teaching in Towns and Villages: Rural Hygiene. London: Spottiswoode, 1894.

Letters, etc., written by Florence Nightingale and photographs of important places and people in her life. Thirty-four pieces in one box. Special Collections, Milbank Memorial Library, Teachers College, Columbia University, New York.

Notes on Hospitals. London: Parker, 1858.

Notes on Nursing: What It Is and What It Is Not. New York: Appleton-Century, 1946.

Richards, L.E. (Ed.) "Letters of Florence Nightingale," *Yale Review.* 24 (1934): 326–347.

Sattin, Anthony. (Ed.) *Letters from Egypt: A Journey on the Nile, 1849–1850.* New York: Weidenfeld and Nicholson, 1987.

Seymer, L.R. (Ed.) *Selected Writings of Florence Nightingale.* New York: Macmillan, 1954.

Books About Florence Nightingale and Her Era:

Baly, Monica E. *Florence Nightingale and the Nursing Legacy.* London: Croom Helm, 1986.

Cook, Sir Edward. *The Life of Florence Nightingale.* 2 volumes. London: Macmillan, 1914.

Goldie, S.M. (Ed.) *I Have Done My Duty: Florence Nightingale in the Crimean War, 1854–56.* Iowa City: University of Iowa Press, 1987.

Howe, Julia Ward. *Reminiscences.* Boston: Houghton-Mifflin, 1900.

Morton, A.L. *A People's History of England.* London: Lawrence and Wishart, 1945.

Nutting, M.A. *Adelaide Nutting Historical Collection.* New York: Teachers College and the School of Nursing, Columbia University.

O'Malley, I.B. *Florence Nightingale, 1820–1856.* London: Thornton Butterworth, 1931.

Russell, William Howard. *Russell's Despatches from the Crimea, 1854–1856.* London: Andre Deutsch, 1966.

Strachey, Lytton. *Queen Victoria*. New York: Harcourt, Brace, 1921.

Summers, Anne. *Angels and Citizens: British Women as Military Nurses, 1854–1914*. New York: Routledge, 1988.

Woodham-Smith, Cecil. *Florence Nightingale*. New York: Atheneum, 1983.

Books for Young Readers:

Cooper, Lettice. *The Young Florence Nightingale*. New York: Roy, 1960.

Harmelink, Barbara. *Florence Nightingale: Founder of Modern Nursing*. New York: Franklin Watts, 1969.

Wyndham, Lee. *Florence Nightingale: Nurse to the World*. New York: World, 1969.

Index

Page numbers for illustrations are in italics.

About the Author

Beatrice Siegel is the author of *Sam Ellis's Island*, a Library of Congress Children's Book of the Year, *Cory: Corazon Aquino and the Philippines*, and *George and Martha Washington at Home in New York*, as well as many other distinguished biographies and works of history for young readers. She lives in New York City with her husband.

SCHOLASTIC BIOGRAPHY

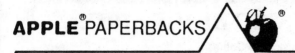

APPLE® PAPERBACKS

Pick an Apple and Polish Off Some Great Reading!

BEST-SELLING APPLE TITLES

❏ MT43944-8	**Afternoon of the Elves** Janet Taylor Lisle	$2.75
❏ MT43109-9	**Boys Are Yucko** Anna Grossnickle Hines	$2.95
❏ MT43473-X	**The Broccoli Tapes** Jan Slepian	$2.95
❏ MT40961-1	**Chocolate Covered Ants** Stephen Manes	$2.95
❏ MT45436-6	**Cousins** Virginia Hamilton	$2.95
❏ MT44036-5	**George Washington's Socks** Elvira Woodruff	$2.95
❏ MT45244-4	**Ghost Cadet** Elaine Marie Alphin	$2.95
❏ MT44351-8	**Help! I'm a Prisoner in the Library** Eth Clifford	$2.95
❏ MT43618-X	**Me and Katie (The Pest)** Ann M. Martin	$2.95
❏ MT43030-0	**Shoebag** Mary James	$2.95
❏ MT46075-7	**Sixth Grade Secrets** Louis Sachar	$2.95
❏ MT42882-9	**Sixth Grade Sleepover** Eve Bunting	$2.95
❏ MT41732-0	**Too Many Murphys** Colleen O'Shaughnessy McKenna	$2.95

Available wherever you buy books, or use this order form.

Scholastic Inc., P.O. Box 7502, 2931 East McCarty Street, Jefferson City, MO 65102

Please send me the books I have checked above. I am enclosing $_____ (please add $2.00 to cover shipping and handling). Send check or money order — no cash or C.O.D.s please.

Name_____ Birthdate_____

Address _____

City_____ State/Zip _____

Please allow four to six weeks for delivery. Offer good in the U.S.A. only. Sorry, mail orders are not available to residents of Canada. Prices subject to change.

APP693